Chakras

Awaken Your Seven Chakras Through Meditation To Immediately Experience Energy

(Its Crucial Role In Maintaining The Health And Balance Of Our Bodies)

Jefferey Meadows

TABLE OF CONTENT

Does Yoga Help To Balance The Chakras?............1

Energy Flow In The Body..7

The Sacral Chakra...18

The 7 Chakras 29

Sacral Yoga Postures And Flows............................47

Indigo..63

Clairvoyance Activation: Having Visions 66

Guided Meditation Planning..................................80

General Guidelines For Determining Which Chakra To Activate...90

Improve Your Spiritual Vision Using The Third Eye Chakra... 102

The Relationship Between The Throat Chakra 111

The Significance Of Energy Hubs....................... 122

Fifth Chakra 127

Does Yoga Help To Balance The Chakras?

Yoga is one of the most prevalent methods for bringing your chakras back into alignment. Tantric yoga is one of the finest, but any form of yoga can be extremely beneficial and ensure that you obtain the desired results from obstructed or damaged chakras. This chapter will spend a considerable amount of time discussing tantric yoga, as it is the style that most closely relates to the chakras. However, if you want to learn a little beginning yoga to get started, this can also do marvels for the chakras.

According to tantric yogis, yoga can help you strengthen your chakras because it enables you to experience specific life changes. Consequently, you are able to sense the inner changes that are occurring. This can be visualized by imagining the chakras as a rotating wheel, as they entail a convergence of the energies, emotions, and thoughts associated with their particular physical bodies. You will learn to differentiate your emotions from reality, your fear from confidence, and your aversions from your desires whenever this occurs. Yoga will be able to restore order to all of this, and if any of your chakras are blocked, it will be able to unblock them so that you can attain your full potential.

The top yoga positions for each chakra

Even as a novice, you will fall in love with how wonderful yoga makes your energy feel and how simple it is to learn. Spending just a few minutes per day on yoga is often sufficient to help you regain the energy and equilibrium you need to feel wonderful in no time. Among the finest poses you can practice for your chakras are the following:

The Warrior I is an excellent pose for establishing a stronger connection to the earth. It will provide a solid foundation for the foot. This pose will provide a nice stretch for the pelvis, which can help to discharge some stagnant energy from the root chakra.

Bound Angle Pose: This is an excellent pose for opening the pelvis and bringing awareness to the pelvic region. Stretching this groin will aid in the discharge of this tension and improve the functioning of this chakra.

This posture, also known as the Boat Pose, will be utilized to stimulate your third chakra. This one will be located at the solar plexus, and Navasana will activate the fire from Manipura while also assisting us in connecting to our own center.

This posture is excellent for expanding the heart center. It is common for many individuals to secure their souls while also closing them off to vulnerability, but this will restrict our daily experiences. When we use the Camel Pose to balance our heart chakra, we open our hearts in order to receive and give more affection.

Fish Pose is an excellent posture for releasing the pharynx chakra. When we take the time to extend out our throats, it will be simpler for us to freely express ourselves through our own voices, rather than relying on others to make all of our decisions.

Child's pose: this is a really basic pose, but it will stimulate the intuition center in our bodies by connecting the third eye to the floor. By activating and bringing awareness to this chakra, we will have greater access to our profound inner wisdom. You can also position the first under the third eye while performing this pose to stimulate the brain further.

Headstand: This pose is more difficult for many people to perform, but it will activate the crown chakra because it applies pressure to the top of the skull. This is your portal to universal consciousness, and when we stimulate it, we draw attention to this region, making it simpler to connect with our ideal higher selves.

To maximize the benefits of these exercises, it is advisable to perform them in succession as your regimen. Holding each pose for approximately ten deep breaths before moving on can assist you in holding them long enough to obtain the necessary stretch before moving on to the next pose. It is also recommended that you go through this list two or three times, or even more if the issues with some of your chakras are particularly severe. This is only a seven-move sequence, so it won't take too much of your time and will make you feel significantly better in no time.

Obviously, if you are pressed for time and feel that only one or two chakras are causing you difficulty, you can choose the position that you believe will be most effective. A minute or so in each pose can do wonders for opening that chakra and making it feel better than it did previously. It is essential to listen to your body and understand when it requires you to make adjustments or when one of your chakras is not functioning properly.

The chakras and yoga were developed along the same line of thought and in the same tradition many years ago, which is why it is often expected that you will engage in some yoga practice if you want your chakras to become more balanced. Yoga is a relatively simple form of exercise, and whether you incorporate it into your daily meditation and rest or use it after grueling practices, it will still provide the desired benefits. Try at least a few of these poses occasionally, and you will be amazed at the difference it can make in your overall health.

Energy Flow In The Body

You may be under the impression that every living and nonliving thing in the world consists solely of its corporeal substance. However, this is not wholly accurate. Let us return to the fundamentals of physics and biology that you may have learned in school, where you would have learned that energy is present in every entity in the universe. This may make you question how this is true. You may recall learning that matter is present everywhere. This brings us to the following question. What actually is the issue? Simply stated, matter is composed of molecules. And these molecules are composed of atoms, each of which can be composed of either protons or electrons, the two opposing forces. When these atoms charged with opposing forces collide, they produce energy, which is present in every living thing on the planet. It creates a dynamic and pulsating electromagnetic energy field. This vitality within your body is known as the subtle body. The so-called subtle body interacts with the corporeal body and passes through only specific body regions. The regions through which the subtle body circulates are known as the chakras.

Your body is composed of various chakras, which are separated into major and minor chakras. There are seven main chakras that are crucial to our well-being. The chakras interact with the various organs present in our body and assist in distributing positive energy throughout the body, as well as removing unwanted or negative energy. You must remember that these chakras are vitally essential and that you must treat them with care and reverence. To ensure not only your physical but also your mental well-being, you will also need to begin working towards balancing these chakras. You will learn everything about this topic in the following chapters.

Relationship between the Aura and the Chakras

Are you familiar with the term aura? It is probable that the majority of us have encountered this term at some point. How many of you have seen the painting depicting the Buddha meditating beneath the Body Gaya? If you had, you would have noticed a rainbow-colored halo surrounding his body in the painting. This is known as one's aura. And every person has an aura that exists in their body and adheres to them. Your aura's ability to disseminate is contingent on how much energy you have in your body. Aura also helps you replenish any energy you may have expended throughout the day.

A person will only be able to see the aura if they have the sensitivity to perceive this radiance. Those who can perceive an individual's aura believe that it can provide insight into not only the body but also the psyche. They will be able to see how your health is affected by the environment and how the environment effects you. Not only this, but also your sentiments and the way in which they change based on the given circumstances. Every individual has a unique aura, so no two individuals can have the same aura. You may witness a different color emanating from a person's aura, but another observer may pick up on a different hue. Consider that you may perceive your aura to be blue, whereas another person may perceive your aura to be red or even green. Everyone has distinct perceptions, so there are differences in this.

How to identify and interpret the human aura

Have you ever seen a painting or photograph depicting a deity? You may observe that a radiance emanates from their body, almost as if they were emitting light from within. This illumination is known as the aura. Likewise, even humans have an aura surrounding them, which is a field of energy. Simply put, a person's aura is the mirror that allows one to observe the energy flow within their body. The circulation of this energy defines your existence. Every magnet, for instance, has a magnetic field that surrounds it; this magnetic field is the magnet's aura. And similarly, your aura can be compared to a magnetic field that surrounds you. Your aura is made up of all the different energies that circulate through your body. Each individual possesses multiple auras, which are responsible for defining their characteristics.

Different colors will be used to depict your energy field. The color of the aura field you project will depend on the subtle energy that circulates within your body. The hues vary based on your individual experiences and emotions.

The primary aura

You must have seen the painting of Lord Buddha seated beneath Bodh Gaya; in this painting, a brilliant white light encircles his body. This will be his primary aura. Similarly, each of us has a primary aura, which is responsible for forming the bonds of various hues that surround the body. Examining one's aura reveals that each of the body's chakras is associated with a distinct color. In addition, the energy produced by these chakras is reflected in our primary aura. The primary aura is the aura that is attached to our epidermis, and it never leaves the body except at night. The color of your primary aura depends on the equilibrium of all the other energies generated by the chakras in your body.

The aura of ethereal radiation

This may be of interest to all film enthusiasts who are reading it. How many of you have seen 'Knowing' starring Nicholas Cage? If you didn't know, the narrative of this film is quite straightforward: it's about aliens who cause devastation. And in the denouement, these aliens land their spacecraft on Earth. These entities were enveloped by an almost filmy white luminescence. This light is their etheric aura, and humans have an aura that is remarkably similar. While you are sleeping, your etheric aura is active. Typically, we expend the majority of our energy during the day and deplete our energy reserves. During a restful night's sleep, the etheric aura assists in recharging all of the energy you would have expended during the day, as well as replenishing your energy reserves. The recharging cycle of the etheric aura begins the moment you fall asleep. And you are not required to prepare for any of this to occur.

Are Chakras our body's blueprint?

There are numerous organs within your body, and each of these organs is vital to your survival, not to mention that they assist you in carrying out all of your essential functions. Likewise, the chakras present in your body serve as the blueprint for your aura. The enormous quantity of energy they contain enables you to execute all tasks. And various colors represent the vitality they contain. The colors emanate from the point where these chakras are located, and they converge at the base of the vertebrae. The chakras can be viewed as a blueprint of the aura that your body transmits by utilizing these chakras. The chakras contain information about not only your past, but also your present and future. The chakras within your body have an impact on both your mental and physical health. Typically, the chakras use your endocrine system to elicit responses from you.

The different strata of the aura

If you have ever observed a caterpillar larva that has cocooned itself, you know that the larva undergoes metamorphosis and transforms into a butterfly that emerges from its cocoon and flies away. In a similar manner, the energy field present in your body envelops you. The aura is comparable to a cocoon that envelops your body. The majority of spiritual healers believe that the aura is merely a layer formed by the merging of electromagnetic fields. The energy tends to move away from the body as it diminishes. When viewed as a single entity, this field resembles a rainbow. There are multiple hues that appear to swirl together. When a person has attained spiritual enlightenment, their aura has a tendency to appear white in color.

The Sacral Chakra

Also known as the water chakra or tenderness - 'In your own residential location'

This strikes a balance between sexuality, emotion, desire, imagination, intuition, and self-worth. If it is blocked, you might feel emotionally explosive, drained of energy, and isolated. Physically, it can result in kidney and uterine problems, lower back pain, impotence, and prostate issues.

Once our survival requirements have been met by balancing the root chakra, we can move on to learning how to appreciate life, learning how to receive and give delight without remorse, transitioning from what is required for fundamental survival to what makes life worthwhile.

This chakra is represented by a six-petaled, orange-red Lotus flower containing a second lotus flower and a crescent moon pointing upwards.

It is associated with the gonads, which are the ovaries and testes.

The sacral chakra is situated one inch below the navel and above the genitalia; its color is orange.

Orange is produced by combining red and yellow and is located next to red on the electromagnetic spectrum, making it a warm and stimulating hue. It is the color of happiness and vitality, and it can even help alleviate depression. It is related to zeal, autonomy, self-assurance, and sociability

Diet plays a significant role in our health and wellbeing. In the end, you truly are what you consume.

The sacral chakra is associated with citrus foods, such as carrots, sweet potatoes, apricots, pumpkin, and peaches, as well as fluids.

You can use crystals such as carnelian, orange calcite, aragonite, amber, and orange sapphire to balance the energy of the sacral chakra when you work with healing crystals.

Rose, jasmine, sandalwood, ginger, ylang ylang, and citrus have an affinity for the sacral chakra if you enjoy working with aromatherapy fragrances and massage.

The energy emanating from the sacral chakra.

The sacral chakra represents the sanctity and delicacy of our residence, which is referred to as our domicile.

Vital to survival are the root chakra's fundamental health and solid foundations, but the ability to appreciate life is what transforms mere survival into living.

In recent years, a dreadful and depressing idiom has gained considerable popularity. "Life is difficult, then you die"

It's such an extremely negative view on life that is seen as a joke. This attitude, however, will generate its own downward spiral of negativity. You will actively seek for things to go awry, and you will anticipate being disappointed, let down, and wretched.

Our attitudes toward accomplishment and enjoyment are influenced by the sacral chakra. It influences our relationships, sexuality, and outlook on desire and passion.

It has an effect on the body's fluid systems, fertility, the reproductive system, the kidneys, and the bladder.

When the sacral chakra is closed or rotating too quickly, you may have significant issues with your attitude toward pleasure, either closing yourself off from it wholly in a very puritanical manner, viewing pleasure as a vice, or, on the other hand, pursuing pleasure for its own sake. Either of these attitudes is extremely toxic and can lead to severe emotional and physical problems, such as emotional immaturity, a tendency to feel extremely envious, or, on the opposite end of the spectrum, a tendency to feel extremely remorseful.

Physically, an unbalanced sacral chakra can result in kidney issues, uterine and prostate issues, irritable bowel syndrome, middle or lower back discomfort, and issues with fertility or impotence.

We have developed a very toxic attitude toward pleasure in the West, regarding it as immoral, expecting to suffer in life, and believing that only hard labor and sacrifice will lead to success. This disposition indicates an unbalanced sacral chakra.

Women can develop a martyr complex when they are expected to place everyone else before themselves, including their children, partners, and coworkers. A woman who prioritizes herself is considered egotistical and even unnatural, but everyone must be able to care for themselves and appreciate life.

Insofar as you take care of your own health and happiness, placing yourself first puts you in a much better and stronger position to be able to care for others.

The sacral chakra is especially associated with our sexual orientation. When the sacral chakra is out of balance, we have a dysfunctional relationship with sexuality and passion. Of course, associating sex in one's consciousness with remorse, immorality, or suffering will not result in pleasurable sexual encounters or a fulfilling sex life with a loving partner.

The other extreme is to pursue pleasure solely for its own sake, becoming a pleasure addict without ever attaining contentment on deeper levels. This can manifest in our sexual behavior, such as engaging in short-term or dysfunctional relationships, but it can also manifest in other areas of pleasure-seeking, such as our incessant search for new methods and new things that will make us joyful but never do.

It can involve continually acquiring new possessions. The next new thing that you must have, but that loses its appeal as soon as you acquire it: a new car, a new pocketbook, a new job, or a new partner. This is a very draining and negative way to live, and you will radiate negativity, attracting those who will affirm your belief that your life cannot improve and that you are simply unlucky. No matter what you do, you will not win life's lottery.

A balanced sacral chakra enables you to interact with others in a healthy and constructive manner.

When you have a positive outlook on enjoyment and pleasure-giving, you will radiate that outlook. You will be a pleasant person to be around, so people will want to spend time with you.

A person with a balanced sacral chakra tends to focus on the positive rather than the negative, the good rather than the evil. If they performed a SWOT analysis (Strength Opportunity Weakness Threat) on their lives, they would focus on their strengths and opportunities as opposed to their weaknesses and threats. Rather than viewing a problem as an obstacle, they view it as a challenge and concentrate on the opportunities it presents.

A balanced sacral chakra allows for an ardent, sensual, and satisfying sexual existence, but it is more than that. It enables you to be open and honest in your relationship, to respect your companion, to experience emotional stability, and to have a healthy relationship to delight and intimacy.

A person who has a balanced sacral chakra can appreciate life in general. When adversity strikes, they can anticipate a time when conditions will improve. They are able to appreciate the little things in life instead of always seeking the major reward because they are aware that winter will eventually transform into spring. People are more inclined to spend time with them because they are pleasant company.

Thus, a prosperous and joyful existence becomes a self-fulfilling prophecy.

The sacral chakra impacts.

This chakra is associated with sexual energy and influences attraction, emotion, vitality, desire, creativity, intuition, self-worth, sexuality, the reproductive system, and all fluid functions of the body, including the bladder and kidneys, prostate, lymph nodes, and adipose deposits.

Once our survival requirements have been met, we can move on to learning how to appreciate life, learning how to receive and give enjoyment guilt-free, transitioning from what is required for fundamental survival to those aspects of life that make it worthwhile to live.

When the sacral chakra is closed or rotating too quickly, you may have significant issues with your attitude toward pleasure, either closing yourself off from it wholly in a very puritanical manner, viewing pleasure as a vice, or, on the other hand, pursuing pleasure for its own sake. Either of these attitudes is extremely toxic and can lead to severe emotional and physical problems, such as emotional immaturity, a tendency to feel extremely envious, or, on the opposite end of the spectrum, a tendency to feel extremely remorseful.

Physically, an unbalanced sacral chakra can result in kidney issues, uterine and prostate issues, irritable bowel syndrome, middle or lower back discomfort, and issues with fertility or impotence.

In Balance

The sacral chakra is the center of spirituality. When it is balanced and activated, vitality and health will circulate through you. You have a healthy self-image, direction, emotional stability, and relationship with desire, delight, and intimacy.

You are trustworthy and expressive, attuned to your emotions and feelings, and able to see the bright side of situations.

The sacral chakra's equilibrium enables you to find satisfaction in life by approaching things with enthusiasm, being eager to appreciate life, and focusing on the positive aspects of existence.

People with a balanced sacral chakra are often viewed as 'fortunate,' but this is because they tend to focus on the positives rather than the negatives in a given situation.

Out of proportion

Imbalance can manifest as impotence, frigidity, or a sexual addiction, emotional immaturity, a propensity for envy, dread of intimacy, remorse, and obsession. You may experience emotional volatility, fatigue, or feelings of isolation.

Physically, it may cause kidney and uterine disorders, irritable bowel syndrome, lower or middle back discomfort, impotence and prostate issues, and infertility.

The 7 Chakras

When conversing with a spiritual healer, chiropractor, acupuncturist, or yoga instructor, the term "chakra" is frequently employed. However, it is not commonly used in the modern world. Many people dislike the word "chakra" because it sounds too "hippie" or "new age."

Numerous individuals believe that these chakras are not genuine and do not exist. However, chakras are genuine and have a significant impact on your existence, whether or not you believe in them. They have an effect on your vitality level. In addition, they govern your emotions, health, and the character of your life and relationships.

However, what are chakras? Where are they positioned, and why should you care?

Chakras are the body's energy centers or fields. These energy fields operate predominantly on your spirit or non-physical body, but they do correspond with areas of your physical body.

The chakras are spinning spheres that transfer energy up and down the body. They are connected to specific organs and glands and are responsible for the distribution of the life force known as "chi/qi" or "prana."

The chakras serve as the basis of your energy ecosystem. This ecosystem's flaws or deficiencies can have a negative impact on various aspects of your existence. When one or two of your chakras are blocked, you will experience physical and psychological problems.

There are numerous energy centers in the human body, but seven main chakras are located from the base of the vertebrae to the crown of the cranium.

Solar Plexus Chakra (Manipura)

This chakra is located between the clavicle and navel in the upper abdomen or abdominal region. This chakra governs your confidence in yourself. Various organs, including the spleen, liver, small intestine, and pancreas, are associated with it.

People with a balanced solar plexus chakra have the vitality of a child. They are receptive, stress-free, and respectful of authority. They possess a robust sense of community and teamwork. They also possess honesty and determination. They are also intellectual and practical.

This chakra's governing element is fire. When this chakra is out of balance, you will experience "gut feelings" that may cause you to feel anxious or agitated. Additionally, you will have impaired memory and concentration.

If you're in need of a fast confidence boost, you must calibrate this chakra. This chakra's equilibrium allows you to feel centered in spirit, body, and intellect. It also helps you develop a stronger connection with your intuition or inner feelings, allowing you to act appropriately and with assurance.

This chakra is associated with a number of gemstones and minerals, including malachite, topaz, and orange calcite.

Root Chakra (Mooladhara)

The first chakra, the root chakra, is colored red. It is the most concentrated of the seven chakras. It is located at the base of the vertebrae, just above the tailbone, and is composed of earth.

This chakra corresponds to the bladder, kidneys, pelvis, thighs, and vertebrae.

This chakra is related to various jewels and stones, including fire agate, black tourmaline, bloodstone, hematite, and tiger's eye.

Sacral Chakra (Swadhisthana)

The second chakra is the sacral one. It is situated below the belly button and above the pelvic bone. Its orange hue is linked to a variety of organs, including the uterus, prostate, testes, ovaries, intestines, abdomen, lower sacrum, and bladder.

Individuals with a balanced sacral chakra are typically ardent, joyful, energetic, athletic, self-confident, and constructive. When this chakra is in harmony, your body moves with ease. You enjoy excellent health as well. You are motivated and intent on achieving your personal objectives.

When your sacral chakra is in harmony, you interact with others in a harmonious manner and enjoy joyful, mutually supportive relationships. You'll feel gratified, and you do not sense any void.

This chakra governs your capacity to experience enjoyment and delight. Additionally, it affects sexuality, desire, and libido. You will feel like an erotic deity or god when your sacral chakra is balanced. You would have sexual confidence and a fulfilling sex life.

Numerous gemstones, including citrine, carnelian, coral, and moonstone, are associated with this chakra.

Heart Chakra (Anahata)

The fourth chakra is the emotional center. It resides in the middle of the thorax. This chakra governs the immune system, lungs, thymus organs, heart, and blood circulation. In addition, it determines our capacity to give and receive unconditional affection.

Those whose heart chakra is in harmony are compassionate and considerate. They also possess the ability to readily acclimate to change. They are tranquil, affable, amusing, and joyful.

However, individuals with a hyperactive heart chakra are codependent. They are typically overly concerned with the emotional requirements of others, to the extent of neglecting their own. They love without discrimination. This could result in harassment and discontentment.

Those whose chakras are out of balance are apathetic, unforgiving, despondent, detached, mistrustful, and detached. In addition, they experience physical symptoms including pneumonia, asthma, respiratory difficulties, upper back discomfort, and premature aging.

Green jasper, emerald, jade, green tourmaline, rhodonite, green moldavite, dioptase, peridot, moss agate, aventurine, and chrysoprase are gemstones associated with this chakra.

Visuddha Chakra (Throat Chakra)

As its name suggests, this chakra is located in the pharynx. It is linked to self-expression, originality, and the truth. This chakra enables you to express your thoughts and emotions. It is blue in color, and air is its governing element.

When this chakra is in harmony, you can readily express your emotions. You can express your beliefs, ideas, and emotions with ease. You are also extremely creative; you croon, draw, write poetry, and carve wood.

When your vocal chakra is out of balance, you will likely lie habitually. Therefore, if you have a propensity for deceiving yourself and others and have difficulty distinguishing between truth and falsehoods, you may have an unbalanced throat chakra.

This chakra is related to a variety of gemstones and crystals, including aquamarine, turquoise, lapis lazuli, and sodalite.

Third Eye Chakra (Ajna)

This chakra is located between the eyebrows on the cranium. Its indigo hue represents our capacity to see the broad picture and make wise decisions.

When this chakra is out of balance, you experience tension easily and your judgment is frequently impaired. You also struggle with organizing your thoughts and making sensible decisions.

This chakra is linked to various crystals and precious stones, including purple amethyst, tanzanite, danburite, Satya Loka quartz, herderite, scolecite, petalite, and phenacite.

Crown Chakra (Sahasrara)

This chakra resides at the crown of the cranium. It signifies your spirituality and enables you to experience joy. It symbolizes enlightenment, inner calm, clarity, and universal wisdom. It is purple in color and is governed by ether or space.

When this chakra is in harmony, you can comprehend things in a much broader context. You believe you are always in the ideal location at the ideal time. Additionally, you'll feel empowered and joyous.

When this chakra is out of balance, you will experience a variety of psychological and physical problems, including depression, confusion, mental disconnection, schizophrenia, epilepsy, light sensitivity, migraines, and neurological disorders. An unbalanced Crown chakra also causes you to become egocentric, materialistic, and dominant. Therefore, if you are overbearing or enjoy purchasing at upscale department stores, you may have an unbalanced crown chakra.

Crystals such as rainbow quartz, amethyst, black merlinite, beta quartz, hyalite opal, nirvana quartz, clear quartz, howlite, rutilated quartz, and sugilite are associated with this chakra.

The seven main chakras are the root chakra, solar plexus chakra, sacral chakra, heart chakra, pharynx chakra, third eye chakra, and crown chakra. There are actually 12 chakras in some chakra systems, including the earth star chakra, navel chakra, causal chakra, soul star chakra, and stellar gateway.

Spirit Star

The eighth chakra, known as the soul star chakra, purifies and heals the lower body. It is located approximately 18 inches above the crown chakra and is known as the soul seat. This chakra controls your life mission.

Terrene Chakra

The ninth chakra is the earth chakra, which is located one foot below the surface of the planet. This chakra maintains your connection to the planet. It is the source of the potent Kundalini force.

Solar Chakra

This chakra is the eleventh. This chakra connects you to the sun-dwelling deities and plays a significant role in your spiritual evolution.

Cosmic Chakra

This chakra is connected to the galactic system through the palm of your hand.

Therefore, if you want to get the most out of life, you should cleanse your energy centers and ensure that they are operating properly.

How Chakras Function

We all have both a corporeal body and an energy body. Auras and meridian lines are components of our energy constitution. Auras are non-physical energy fields that encircle a person and disclose their emotions, thoughts, and desires. A person with specialized training in the healing arts is typically able to perceive the various colors of your aura.

A meridian line, on the other hand, is a path through which the life force known as "qi" or "chi" flows. It is frequently employed in Chinese medicine. When you visit an acupuncturist or a spiritual healer, you will frequently hear these terms.

When the body is cut open, these auras and meridian lines are not visible, but you know they are there. When you are familiar with auras, you understand that they are affected by positive and negative vibrations. Therefore, if you receive a positive or negative impression from someone, you may be sensing his aura. Because these vibrations are contained in a person's energy, speaking with them elicits particular emotions.

Chakras, like auras and meridian lines, are part of the body's energetic anatomy. They function as an energy orb that spins like a wheel to equitably distribute your energy throughout your body.

These chakras cannot be seen on an X-ray because they are not part of the corporeal body. They are a component of our consciousness and interact with the corporeal body through the various organs. Each chakra is associated with a specific endocrine gland and a plexus of nerves.

Are certain chakras more vital than others? The response is no. Each chakra is of equal importance. To live a healthy existence, you must balance all of your body's chakras.

Equally essential as the spiritual function of the crown chakra and the transcendent aspect of the heart chakra is the root chakra's function of grounding.

To maximize your mental and physical functions, you must achieve chakra balance and address your fundamental, relational, creative, safety, belongingness, and self-actualization needs.

Chakras and Your Physical Structure

We are all composed of energy. Therefore, if your energy centers are impeded, you will suffer from a variety of maladies. When one or two of your chakras are not rotating, the energy is not distributed evenly throughout your body, which may impair the performance of certain organs.

For instance, the heart chakra is located in the thorax and encompasses the heart and respiratory system. Consequently, if your heart chakra is not rotating, you will have heart and circulation issues. Additionally, you are susceptible to respiratory illnesses and allergies.

The throat chakra is responsible for the pharynx and mouth. Consequently, if it is not functioning properly, you will develop mouth ulcers, irritated throats, and thyroid issues.

Many Western medical practitioners do not believe this, but your chakras can influence the functions of your body. Unbalanced chakras can inflict havoc on your life, whereas balanced chakras can optimize your health and vitality.

Chakras and Affect

Not only do chakras signify your physical body, but also your emotions and portions of your consciousness. When there is tension in a portion of your consciousness, you will sense it in the chakra associated with that portion.

For instance, if your partner breaks up with you, you will experience discomfort in your heart or bosom. You will feel as though you cannot breathe. When anxious about something, the bladder becomes feeble and the legs shake.

When the tension persists, physical symptoms may manifest.

The Chakras and Life Satisfaction

The chakras influence not only your physical body, but also your mental health and the character of your life as a whole. Consequently, if a portion of your life seems off or if something in your life is not functioning, one of your chakras may be blocked.

When one or two of your chakras are blocked, some aspects of your life may be thriving, while others may be struggling. For instance, your career may be thriving, but you may struggle to maintain healthy relationships.

If you have difficulty paying your obligations but are spiritual, kind, and compassionate, you may have blocked chakras.

When your chakras are not functioning properly, you experience a sense of imbalance. Your subconscious informs you that there is a problem.

The chakras symbolize who you are, including your intellect, emotions, creativity, spirituality, sexuality, vocations, values, and beliefs. Therefore, if your chakras are unbalanced, you will lose perspective on a portion of your life. You may develop psychological issues such as depression, anxiety, hallucinations, or even a nervous collapse.

What Causes Chakra Obstructions?

Several factors can cause chakra obstructions, including one's belief system, career, dwelling circumstance, financial situation, and relationships. Traumatic events such as abuse, an accident, or the death of a loved one can also result in chakra obstructions. Negative emotions such as anxiety, hostility, tension, and terror can also throw off the equilibrium of your chakras.

For instance, physical and emotional maltreatment by a former companion may cause an imbalance in the heart chakra. You may have closed yourself off to prospective romantic prospects. You may also frequently experience feelings of emptiness.

Your root chakra represents the basis of your existence. Therefore, if your parents did not have enough money when you were a child and did not provide enough for you, you will likely experience a blocked root chakra. You may continuously fret that you lack sufficient resources. You may also be perpetually concerned about finances.

Chakra openings and closings

The opening and closure of your chakras function similarly to an energetic defense mechanism. When you undergo a traumatic or negative experience, the corresponding chakra will close to keep the negative energy out. If you adhere to low-frequency emotions such as wrath, remorse, or blame, your chakras will become blocked.

Long-term retention of the following low-frequency emotions can induce chakra blockage:
- Anger
- Pain
- Resentment
- Jealousy

Subversive hostility
- Grief

- Hopelessness
- Sadness

- Regret
- Pessimism
- Worry
- Blame
- Discouragement

- Shame
- Powerlessness
- Depression
- Disappointment
- Frustration
- Despair
- Guilt

The following positive or high-frequency emotions can increase your vibrations and assist in the opening of your chakras:
- Love
- Joy
- Acceptance
- Eagerness
- Optimism
- Passion
- Positive Outlook
- Contentment
- Faith
- Belief

Therefore, to maintain the balance of your chakras, you must abandon egoism. You must decide to act lovingly.
Chakras and Sensitives

The individuals who must open the chakras are known as empaths. They are extremely sensitive individuals. They readily absorb the energy of others, making public spaces overwhelming. They also recognize when someone is not being truthful with them. They are imaginative and have an intense need for solitude. They feel feeble when subjected to noxious individuals.

Empaths must protect and balance their chakras and tote protective stones such as rose quartz, black tourmaline, amethyst, and malachite. These stones serve to restore emotional equilibrium and eliminate anxiety and negative energy.

Sacral Yoga Postures And Flows

Want to attain greater holistic health and well-being by balancing your sacral chakra? Yoga could be the ideal solution. Yoga's concentration on respiration, meditation, and asanas (or poses) can help you to open and restore your sacral chakra while enhancing your strength, flexibility, and mental clarity.

Yoga is a practice that stimulates the sacral chakra, which serves to harmonize physical and emotional requirements and enhance well-being in numerous ways. In addition, regular yoga practice has been shown to strengthen the immune system, reduce tension and anxiety, and improve sleep quality, among other benefits.

Therefore, yoga is the optimal method for balancing your sacral chakra and improving your overall health and well-being. With so many diverse styles of practice available today, there is certainly something for every level of yogi.

This chapter will discuss the benefits of yoga for the sacral chakra and provide specific poses and sequences for opening and healing this chakra. In addition, we will offer advice on how to get started with yoga and determine the best approach for you. So, whether you are new to yoga or a seasoned practitioner, there is certain to be something here that will assist you on your path to greater health and wellness.

Benefits of Yoga for Balancing Svadhisthana

Yoga is an effective method for regulating the sacral chakra. Certain yoga poses improve circulation and pelvic mobility, thereby assisting in the release of obstructions that cause an imbalance in the sacral chakra. In addition, breathing exercises and meditation assist in focusing and calming the mind, fostering feelings of safety and security. Incorporate yoga into your daily routine to help maintain a healthy sacral chakra.

Listed below are a few of the numerous advantages yoga provides by balancing the sacral chakra:

Yoga poses and sequences increase circulation, allowing for a more balanced passage of energy throughout the body.

Yoga poses assist in stretching and opening the muscles and joints, thereby increasing flexibility. This is particularly useful for relieving tension in the pelvis and lower back, which are closely associated with the sacral chakra.

Reduced Anxiety and Stress: Yoga can help focus the mind and promote relaxation through breathing exercises, meditation, and concentrated attention. In turn, this decreases levels of tension and anxiety, promoting a sense of well-being.

Improved Sleep Quality Yoga's relaxation techniques improve sleep quality by fostering a sense of calm and serenity prior to bedtime.

Equilibrated Hormones: The endocrine system, which regulates the hormones in the body, is closely associated with the sacral chakra. By keeping this chakra in shape, you can maintain a healthy hormone balance.

Regular yoga practice enhances one's disposition and mental health as a whole. It is likely due to the increased concentration on respiration and meditation, as well as the endorphins released during physical activity.

As you can see, incorporating yoga into your life to balance the sacral chakra has many benefits. The following section will provide specific poses and sequences to help you activate and restore your sacral chakra.

Asanas to Balance and Open the Sacral Chakra

The sacral chakra governs our capacity for interpersonal connection and delight. Asanas, or yoga positions, serve to balance this chakra by opening the pelvis, thighs, abdomen, and lower back and stimulating the passage of energy in those areas. Some of the most effective asanas to open and balance the sacral chakra are the Goddess pose (Utkata Konasana), Reverse Warrior Pose (Viparita Virabhadrasana), Cross-Legged Twist Pose (Parivrtta Sukhasana), Uttanasana (standing forward fold), Marjaryasana (cat and cow pose), and Balasana (child's pose).

By meditating on these postures daily during your practice, you can improve your vitality, pleasure, creativity, intuition, and emotional health. Start incorporating the following asanas into your regular practice immediately if you wish to balance your sacral chakra and enhance your overall health.

Utkata Konasana (Goddess Pose)

Goddess pose is a standing asana that stretches the pelvis, quadriceps, and torso while fortifying the legs and lower back. This pose also stimulates the passage of energy in the sacral region, making it an ideal asana for opening and balancing the sacral chakra. In this pose, maintain a straight spine while moving the pelvis forward and down.

Instructions:

Begin by placing your feet approximately one foot apart and turning your toes outward.

You should bend your knees and lower your pelvis to the earth. Your arms are extended in front of you, and your quadriceps are parallel to the ground.

Feel the stretch in your pelvis and lower back as you hold this position for a few long breaths.

To relinquish the pose, straighten your legs and return to a standing position.

Depending on your flexibility, you can perform this pose with or without aids.

Place a yoga block or a blanket under your heels to protect them from the ground if you experience knee discomfort. If necessary, you can also perform this pose with your back against a wall for added support.

Viparita Virabhadrasana (Reverse Warrior Pose) is an excellent method to extend the pelvis, abdomen, and lower back while also expanding the ribcage. Regular practice of this asana balances the sacral chakra by stimulating energy flow in the pelvis and lower back. As the reverse warrior pose can be executed in a variety of methods to enhance its efficacy, it is an excellent pose for beginners.

Instructions:

Beginning with your ankles together, turn your right foot outward.

Keep your left knee slightly bent and your right leg erect, with the heels of both legs aligned.

Stretch the right side of your body by pointing your right arm straight up toward the ceiling and gently leaning backwards.

Feeling the stretch in your pelvis and abdomen, hold this pose for several breaths.

To relinquish the pose, extend the right leg and return to a standing position.

The key to accurately performing this pose is to maintain an upright spine and a 90-degree bend in the front knee. If additional support is required, the reverse warrior pose can also be performed while seated on a chair. Remember to maintain your shoulders square and aligned over your hips, and avoid shrugging them forward as you recline back.

Cross-Legged Twist Pose (Parivrtta Sukhasana) The cross-legged twist pose is a gentle and relaxing posture that stretches the pelvis, lower back, and abdomen. This essential yoga pose can be executed in a variety of methods, depending on your flexibility. When performed accurately, the cross-legged twist helps to open and balance the sacral chakra, boosting creativity and emotional health.

Begin by assuming a cross-legged seated position on the earth.

Place your right hand on the ground behind you and rotate to the left while peering over your left shoulder.

Feeling the stretch in your pelvis and lower back, hold this pose for several breaths.

To relinquish the pose, untwist your torso and return to a cross-legged seated position.

The cross-legged twist pose is ideal for novices but can also be performed with the assistance of objects if additional support is required. Place a yoga block under your right buttock to help you tilt your pelvic if your hips are tense. Additionally, you may position a blanket under your knees for added comfort.

Uttanasana (Forward Fold from Standing)

The standing forward fold is a straightforward but effective posture for stretching the hamstrings, lower back, and hips. The forward fold is commonly used as a restorative pose at the conclusion of a yoga session, but it also has numerous therapeutic benefits that help to balance the sacral chakra. The standing forward fold is said to enhance creativity and emotional stability.

Beginning with your feet together, steadily bend forward while maintaining a straight back as you lower yourself.

Allow your head and neck to hang freely while pressing your pelvis as far as possible toward the ground.

Feeling the stretch in your hamstrings and lower back, maintain this pose for several breaths.

To relinquish the pose, slowly roll your spine back up to standing and return to the starting position.

If additional support is required, the standing forward fold can also be performed with a yoga block under the wrists. Remember to keep your shoulders relaxed as you descend down and concentrate on keeping your back upright and in alignment with your legs throughout the duration of the pose.

Ardha Matsyendrasana is also known as Half Fish Pose.

Sequencing and Alternative Poses

Once you have learned the basic yoga poses, you can start putting them together into sequences. These sequences can be as simple or as complex as you like, depending on your goals or experience level. You can also use different poses to target specific body areas, like stretching the upper back and shoulders or toning the legs and glutes.

There are many different sequences you can try, but here are a few popular options to get you started:

Sequence 1:

Marjaryasana (Cat and Cow Pose) – 5-10 breaths

Balasana (Child's Pose) – 5-10 breaths

Uttanasana (Standing Forward Fold) – 5-10 breaths

Sequence 2:

Uttanasana (Standing Forward Fold) – 5-10 breaths

Ardha Matsyendrasana (Half Fish Pose) – 5-10 breaths on each side

Paschimottanasana (Seated Forward Fold) – 5-10 breaths

Adding Variety

If you have been practicing yoga for some time, you'll find your body becomes accustomed to doing the same poses in the same order every day. Therefore, it's important to mix things up and add variety to your practice. Here are a few ways that you can do this:

Vary the Order of Your Poses – Do the cat and cow pose first instead of last, or alternate between the standing and seated forward folds.

Add New Poses – If you're feeling adventurous, add new poses to your sequences. There are hundreds of yoga poses to choose from, so you're sure to find some that suit your level and goals.

Hold Poses for Different Lengths of Time – Instead of holding the standing forward fold for a full 5-10 breaths, hold it for just 2 or 3. This will keep your practice interesting and challenging.

Use Props – Props, like yoga blocks or straps, help deepen your stretch or get into poses that would otherwise be difficult.

Practice with a Friend – Practicing with a friend makes your practice more enjoyable and motivating. It's also a great way to learn new poses and get feedback on your form.

Practicing yoga is a great way to improve your flexibility, strength, and overall wellbeing. By adding variety to your practice, you keep your body and mind challenged and maintain your motivation and progress.

Alternate Poses

While the basic yoga poses and sequences are a great starting point, there are many other options for creating your practice. If you're looking for something different, these simple alternatives are some of the most common poses:

Instead of a seated forward fold, try a reclined twist – This pose is a great way to release tension in the lower back and spine.

Instead of the child's pose, try a supported backbend – This pose is a gentle way to open the chest and heart.

Instead of the cat and cow pose, try a spinal roll – This is an easy way to loosen up the spine and release built-up tension in the back, neck, and shoulders.

Instead of a standard side plank, try a dolphin plank – This pose is a great way to build strength in the core and upper body.

Instead of a pose for the shoulders, try a forward fold instead – This is an easy way to release tension in the neck and upper back.

Yoga beyond the Asanas

When many people think of yoga, they often picture standing poses, twists, and extensions - activities that seem to require quite a bit of effort and muscle engagement. However, the truth is that yoga is about far more than mere physical postures. At its heart, yoga is a practice of connecting one's mind and body, developing greater awareness and focus, and ultimately achieving balance and harmony in all aspects of life. This holistic approach has particular resonance in healing the sacral chakra, which runs along the center axis of the lower belly and is associated with pleasure and desire.

Incorporating other practices such as pranayama (breathing exercises), meditation, or mudras into your yoga routine, you help open your body on a deeper level by facilitating flow through this key energy center. Whether you work these elements into your regular asana practice or simply use them as standalone methods for balancing your energy centers, they will help ground you physically while relieving stress and tension. Keeping your sacral chakra open will also allow you to reconnect with your genuine desire for life in all its beauty.

Hopefully, the information presented in this chapter has helped introduce you to the various aspects of yoga and its many benefits, but there is always more to learn. If you're interested in deepening your practice and learning more about yoga's potential for healing and growth, consider enrolling in a yoga teacher training program or seeking other resources to help you on your journey.

Indigo

Indigo, the color of perception and intuition, is a beautiful hue associated with unleashing your imagination. In this chapter, let's gain a greater comprehension of this concept.

Indigo: The Generational Color

In the 1980s and 1990s, it is said, a cohort of "Indigo Children" was born. Not all children born during this period are considered "Indigo Children," but a portion of them are believed to have psychic abilities and are frequently diagnosed with ADD or other cognitive disorders. Who knows if this is true, but indigo does represent intuition and the third vision. It is believed to enhance focus and profound concentration during introspection and to help unlock your state of consciousness. You can see and comprehend things beyond the capacity of your normal senses and gain a deeper understanding of everything.

This dark midnight blue hue also represents authority, dignity, profound sincerity, and integrity. Additionally, it is associated with wisdom, devotion, equity, justice, and impartiality. People who integrate a great deal of indigo into their lives are organized and structured and are incapable of living a chaotic lifestyle.

Color of the Brow Chakra

Indigo is the color of the sixth chakra, the 'brow' chakra, which in Sanskrit is known as the 'ajna' chakra and is located between your eyebrows. It corresponds to your cranium, forehead, brain, pituitary gland, eyes, carotid nerve plexus, and pineal gland on a physical level.

When your brow chakra is primarily active when indigo energy is balanced in your body and environment, you have excellent vision, a healthy metabolism, a healthy thyroid gland, a strong and fit upper body, and healthy teeth. However, when the ajna chakra is occluded, all of these areas become problematic.

On a mental and emotional level, an active ajna chakra and an equilibrium of indigo energy result in a strong memory, sensitivity, intelligence, spirituality, the ability to visualize and comprehend things, endurance, discipline, and fortitude. In contrast, an obstructed brow chakra results in poor memory, a lack of creative imagination, insensitivity, poor decision-making skills, and sociopathic behavior.

To maintain a healthy brow chakra, you must maintain a balance of indigo in your life and surroundings. Additionally, spend 10 minutes per day visualizing indigo light entering and soothing your brow chakra. If you do it daily, you will feel energized and begin to reap its benefits.

Indigo is associated with norms, regulations, culture, tradition, and religion.

Let us now learn more about violet, the final color in the color spectrum.

Clairvoyance Activation: Having Visions

Clairvoyance is the ability to perceive occurrences and other objects that are not visible to others. One of the "clairs" that can be received and developed when the third eye is opened. You can see the past, future, and objects unknown to you in the present with this ability. You can see divine entities and more beyond the persistent illusion of reality. The term clairvoyance is a combination of the French words clair and voyance, which mean "clear" and "vision," respectively. In other terms, it is seeing clearly through objects. People frequently believe that "psychic" and "clairvoyant" are synonymous, but "psychic" is an umbrella term for all preternatural abilities.

As a clairvoyant, you can see a variety of things, including entities and events that have not yet occurred, have already occurred, or are occurring where you are not. Thanks to your awakened third eye, you can see beyond the veil, in a sense.

Telepathy and the Third Eye

The fact is that everyone can be clairvoyant. The only requirement is to open your third sight. The truth is that infants have open third senses and can perceive things that most adults cannot until society teaches them to close down that aspect of themselves, which is unfortunately inevitable. You can thankfully reactivate your third eye and regain your clairvoyance immediately. There is no other method to cultivate this psychic ability. To perceive the unseen, your third eye must be fully open and functioning correctly.

Increasing Clairvoyance

Practice Visualization

Since the majority of visions you will receive will appear in your mind, it is advisable to practice visualization. Take time each day to visualize vivid images or experiences in your mind. Another delightful activity would be to take up any nearby object and examine it closely, noting every last detail. Then, close your eyes and visualize the same object in your mind, attempting to recreate every detail exactly as it is in reality. Start envisioning things that are utterly magnificent and that you've never seen anywhere else once you're comfortable with this. Try to draw them into your mind's eye repeatedly, rather than just once. Do not be astonished if you find yourself fantasizing about something you have created.

Play Extrasensory Games

Games that emphasize visual memory will be of great benefit to you. You could, for instance, observe random objects in your home and then attempt to envision them in various hues or sizes. Consider a loved one and envision them with various complexion or hair tones. During these visualization sessions, it is essential to concentrate on the specifics and not simply let them pass through your mind.

Utilize Crystals

You already know which crystals are ideal for the development of your third vision. These very same crystals will do marvels for your clairvoyance. You are not required to acquire all of them; simply select the ones that most resonate with you. Carry them with you wherever you go, wear them as adornment, or simply meditate with one. Additionally, you can sleep with a crystal under your pillow every night.

Practice Astral Teleportation

Projection is similar to lucid dreaming, with the exception that you are not dreaming but instead entering a completely new world known as the astral plane. To have an easier time projecting into other realms, you must first master lucid dreaming, which we have already covered in this chapter. The wake-up-and-go-back-to-bed method is a straightforward way to leave your body.

First, go to bed and get a few hours of sleep, then rise up a little earlier than usual.

After drinking a glass of water and reading a bit about astral projection, return to bed. You could sleep in a semi-upright position on a recliner instead of your bed, if you prefer.

As you fall back asleep, gently remind yourself of your intention to become conscious of your body as it enters a sleep paralysis state. Tell yourself that you will project.

Stay as still as possible and resist any impulses to move or scratch. These signals your body sends you are designed to determine whether or not your mind is alert. If you pass these tests without responding, your body will enter a state of sleep paralysis to prevent you from acting out your hallucinations.

At some point, you will enter a state that can only be described as the abyss while retaining consciousness of your waking state.

Simply submit to the energy when your body begins to vibrate intensely. Caution: If you've never experienced vibrations before, you may feel apprehensive, but there's no cause for alarm. You are not dying and you are not having a heart attack.

Move these vibratory sensations throughout your entire body with your intention. From the bottoms of the feet to the top of the head, and back again.

After gaining sufficient control over the vibrations, which appear to have diminished slightly, merely roll out of your body. When you attain this stage of astral projection, you will know what to do intuitively, despite the fact that this statement sounds very odd. Similar to how you would get out of bed, roll out.

Suppose you are having trouble leaving your body using this method. Imagine a rope therefore suspended just above your cranium. Reach out, grab the rope, and begin to draw to separate yourself from your physical body.

If you are still having trouble leaving your physical body, you can ask your spirit guides or a higher power for assistance. They are always available to provide aid.

Importantly, she cannot afford to be fearful during astral projection; therefore, you must understand that you are surrounded by light and love. You are always safeguarded and safe.

You cannot succumb or become disoriented through astral projection. Staying out of their bodies long enough to investigate the astral dimension is one of the difficulties novice projectors face. Therefore, you need not worry about never returning. Before commencing this procedure, you may, if it helps, pray to your deity or invoke the power of the universe to protect and safeguard you. If you have a fear of the dark, you should avoid projecting at night. Do so only during the day. The more astral projection and lucid dreaming you practice, the more clairvoyant experiences you will have in your life.

Tips and Techniques for Enhancing Your Clairvoyance

In addition to the practices necessary to open the third eye, you must also consider your mental attitude toward the process and acknowledge that it requires patience, persistence, and effort. Therefore, the following information will assist you on your travels:

- Decide to Believe

Belief in a higher power is non-negotiable for many clairvoyants and has enabled them to continue seeing what they see. They believe that their power comes from a higher domain because this world is not very accepting of matters such as clairvoyance. You must acknowledge that there is more to life than meets the eye and believe in a power greater than yourself. This world may be obscured when you close your eyes, but your inner eye reveals worlds within worlds. The fact that you can conceive it indicates that the world consists of more than the corporeal. Consider the fact that everything we've accomplished or created began with imagination, and you'll realize that the source of all creativity and imagination must contain a great deal more power and knowledge. A belief in a superior power does not necessitate religious practice. It simply recognizes that all existence is governed by an intelligent force far beyond human comprehension.

• Don't React Excessively to What You See

You should not overreact when you see strange things, such as a man hovering with his head nearly severed, or anything else that seems odd. You may observe and acknowledge their presence, but please maintain your composure. You should be aware that they cannot injure you. Remember that you can call upon this higher power to protect you and keep you secure, so long as your faith remains unshakeable. You can develop a relationship with this power through meditation, prayer, and constant mental communication.

• Eradicate anxiety from your mind

Some have a morbid fear of the unknown. Unfortunately, this will affect what they see in their visions because anxiety attracts low-vibration, negative entities that can take advantage of them. Learn to overcome your anxieties. The dread does not exist. It is within you. To eliminate anxiety, you need only refrain from fighting it or arguing with it. That is not the way to proceed, and neither is the censure justified. All you need to do to overcome your anxieties is recognize that you are the source of your fear, worry, and anxiety. Consider the anxiety to be entirely of your own making. You are the creator, so you can transform it into something else. You created this dread, and as its creator, you can eliminate it by choosing to experience love. Instead, you need no justification to experience affection. Simply experience it, and your anxiety will vanish. Love is the weapon used to eliminate dread. Love is a potent transformative agent.

- Give heed to your intuition

You will begin to observe things that are not apparent to others if you have clairvoyance. You have an open third eye if you have had experiences in which you sensed an inner awareness about someone, but chose to disregard it, only to later regret it. When you open your third eye and become clairvoyant, you must pay close attention to your intuition and never disregard its guidance.

•Maintain Your Eyes Open

There are times when you may experience greater presence and stability than usual. Because there is something crucial about that moment that you may not realize at the time, every minute detail of what is occurring around you becomes immediately apparent. When this occurs, halt and take in as much information as you can, because it's probable that an experience will occur much later in life as a result of the current occurrences. Your third eye is roused from its dormancy by your constant heightened awareness of your surroundings. The practice of being observant will flow over into your dream life, which is an additional benefit. In other words, you are more likely to notice when something doesn't make sense, as it often does in dreams, and you can then become lucid and use your dreams to manifest what you want, meditate, or simply have fun.

•Retain a Realistic Perspective

It is common for novice clairvoyants to neglect the distinction between the spirit world and the physical world. Don't make this error. Ground yourself by standing barefoot on the earth, lying on your back on the earth, and employing the pranayama techniques discussed earlier in this book.

Guided Meditation Planning

Although a more transcendent and serene process than exercise, meditation requires preparation. Always seek guidance when beginning meditation. As with physical activity, if you are not adequately primed for meditation, you will either not reap the full benefits of the experience or you will have a terrible one.

Preparation

You can prepare your mind, body, and spirit for guided meditation in several ways. These methods are appropriate for all skill levels, not just novices. When you prepare for meditation, you initiate the flow of positive energy into your body. It prepares your mind to deal with the process and gives your spirit a little more freedom.

First, Know Your Chakras

The greater your understanding of each of your seven Chakras, the greater your ability to awaken or unblock them. Meditation is a potent method for redirecting the flow of energy to each of these energy centers. There are factors that can enhance the transcendence of meditation.

The greater your understanding of what stimulates each Chakra, how they interact, and why they function as they do, the more effective your meditation session will be. For instance, you can stimulate your Throat Chakra by singing in the shower each morning. To stimulate your Heart Chakra throughout the day, you can disseminate compassion or even a genuine smile. There are numerous additional methods for stimulating your Chakras, which we will discuss later.

Step 2 — Identifying the Problem's Cause

Given that some symptoms of a blockage affect more than one Chakra, it can be difficult to identify the underlying cause of a problem. Headaches, digestive disturbances, anxiety, and tension may indicate a blockage in three or four of the seven Chakras. If you are performing targeted guided meditation, you must determine why the Chakra in question is blocked.

Step Three: Stimulate the Energy of the Throat and Heart Chakras

There are activities that can stimulate the passage of energy through your Chakras. Once your Chakras have been opened and rebalanced, you must continue to stimulate them. Maintaining the passage of energy through your Chakra energy system is comparable to staying in shape. If you do not invest the necessary time and effort, they will become blocked or unbalanced.

Regular meditation and understanding the causes of your Chakra obstructions are a good starting point. However, there are a few activities you can do or incorporate into your daily routine to keep them stimulated.

Color

Wearing the color associated with the Chakra that requires additional stimulation is a method of attracting the correct energy. You can light a candle in the color of the corresponding Chakra, such as a green candle for the Heart Chakra or a blue candle for the Throat Chakra.

When taking a bath, you could use candles in these colors (or hues). Soothe yourself in the bath and absorb the color of the glowing candle.

The date of the week

The day of the week can have an effect on your Chakras. On the day associated with each Chakra, wearing the color or igniting the color candles allows the correct energy to circulate. Combining your guided meditation routine with donning the Chakra's color and igniting colored aromatic candles on its associated day will assist you in absorbing the proper Chakra energy.

Exercise

Dancing and singing can be used to stimulate the Throat Chakra by means of movement or exercise. Set your voice free and chant or murmur as loudly as possible. Let your spirit absorb the rhythm as you dance to the tune. You can also utilize the yoga positions lotus or half-lotus while chanting, allowing the vibrations to reverberate through your larynx.

To stimulate the Heart Chakra through movement, the blood must circulate. Concentrate on your respiration while performing aerobic exercises. You can also perform some Yoga using the low lunge pose, which stretches the diaphragm to open the Heart Chakra and allows energy to circulate readily through it.

Meditation Altar

Create a meditation altar adorned with images of the Chakra symbols in their respective colors. In a basin, you may also position fragrant color candles and the crystal or stone associated with the Chakra. This assists you in channeling and visualizing the correct energy by establishing the proper ambiance in your meditation space.

Plants

Even plants have their own vibrations that can resonate with your Chakras' vibrations. Herbs and certain blossoms have the strongest associations with the Chakras and can be used to assist with the awakening, healing, and unblocking of each and every Chakra.

You can consume the herbs and even some flowers (such as roses) as infusions or use them as a seasoning in food or beverages. Or you can simply use the plants to decorate your meditation space.

To cleanse, awaken, or purify the Throat Chakra, you can use any herb with a bluish or purple hue, such as lavender, or any herb that is good for the senses or the nervous system. Mint, juniper, passionflower, rosemary, and poppy are herbs and flora that can be utilized for the Throat Chakra.

To purify, awaken, or detoxify the Heart Chakra, you can use any verdant herb or sustenance. Blood and heart-beneficial herbs will be most beneficial to the Heart Chakra. Rose, jasmine, thyme, basil, chamomile, sage, and cilantro are all herbs and flora that can be used for the Heart Chakra.

solitary reflection

When feeling overburdened, irritated, panicked, apprehensive, or agitated, it is essential to spend time alone. Take a moment to recover your breath and mentally or physically visit your joyful place. Consider your thoughts, emotions, and physical being while seated in silence.

Scents

Incense, scented candles, aromatic botanicals, and potpourri are additional ways to stimulate and direct the energy of your Chakras.

During meditation or on the day of the week associated with a Chakra, you can ignite incense or an aromatic candle. Additionally, you can use essential oils to scent your residence or meditation space.

Gems and minerals

When first acquired, stones and crystals must be purified by rinsing them in clean, clear water. This removes any negative energies from the location where you purchased them.

The stone or crystal can be placed in a basin on your meditation altar. Alternate them for each day of the week and position them near your smoldering scented candle or incense.

During meditation, you can use your cleansed stone if you are feeling extremely blocked. Place the stone on your thigh in the palm of your hand. Feel it grow warmer as you begin to channel the Chakra's energy. Bring the stone or crystal's brilliant color and light up through your Root Chakra and allow it to travel to the Chakra you're working on. Keep the stone or crystal with you for five days after the meditation has concluded.

General Guidelines For Determining Which Chakra To Activate

Step 1: Understand Your Chakras
One of the most essential steps in preparing to activate your chakras is to become familiar with them. Each chakra possesses several distinct qualities that are distinct from the others. Consequently, the method of unlocking them differs greatly. When our chakras are out of balance or obstructed, we might experience feelings of disorientation or exhaustion. We may also become unwell. Know what each chakra represents and the indications that they are blocked or out of balance so that you can tend to them as needed.

Step 2: Determine the Need Level
Due to the fact that you have a total of seven well-known chakras, you must determine which one you wish to address first. It can be difficult to determine which individual requires

assistance the most. Because when one is out of alignment, it influences the others. There are a number of indicators that can be used to identify the problematic chakra. One of the initial stages is to take the chakra test by analyzing all of your body regions to determine which has the most issues.

Check whether you can identify physical distress in the area corresponding to the chakra in question. You can also assess the current state of your life and identify problematic issues, such as financial issues, safety concerns, relationship issues, emotional rollercoaster or lack of motivation, etc. You can also consult a professional in chakra energy healing or an energy-aware close acquaintance or colleague.

Step 3: Activate the Chakra Opening Energy

You have identified the problematic chakra at this point. In addition to planning how to activate the chakra, you must also consider how to restore it. By opening this chakra, you are also balancing the flux (both incoming and outgoing) of your energy and increasing your awareness of its state and variations. The main principle used by professional healers and the majority of energy-conscious individuals is the concept of chakra balancing.

In order to activate a chakra, you will need to perform breathing exercises and physical activities with a primary concentration on the specific location of that chakra. Participate in a healing session (found a professional healer or energy-conscious individual), utilize chakra connection techniques or manipulations (also referred to as "self-healing hands-on technique"), and meditate on the specific chakra location.

While employing any of these techniques to heal your chakra, it is vital to be mindful of the possibility that other things may arise. Consider the issues that caused your chakra to become blocked or out of balance in the first place. This is your opportunity to proactively deal with the increased likelihood of these occurrences. Always take care of yourself by ensuring that you are focused, mindful, and aware of everything that is occurring as you open your chakras.

Check which practice resonates with you or makes the most sense when selecting the most suitable technique for opening the chakras. Determine if you require a meditative or physical practice. You may only have a few minutes, or you may be able to schedule an hour or more of practice time.

Chapter 3: Breathing Techniques to Maintain an Open Chakra

The most effective techniques, such as abdominal respiration, utilize the abdomen to transmit more energy and awareness. Learning and mastering this technique will enhance your overall well-being and health.

You will also learn that remembering how to breathe well is just as essential as inhaling itself. The emphasis should be on the intention to maximize the benefits of correct respiration techniques. During the practice, it is essential to be aware of your respiration, which is equally important for optimizing your mind, physical body, and spirit.

Belly breathing is an effective technique for maximizing your health, increasing your vitality, and bringing greater awareness to your body.

What Does the Belly Breathing Method Involve?

Attach your index fingers and thumbs together and position them just below your navel or in the second chakra region just above your pubic region. Imagine sensing this region as you inhale. By breathing into the abdomen, you will feel richer and deeper. It will also assist in directing your respiration in the proper direction. It is simpler to breathe into the abdomen while lying down or standing up. You can also practice while seated, but it is difficult because you may load your torso rather than your abdomen.

Concentrate on your respiration to ensure that you are filling your abdomen rather than your chest.

It is normal and common to envision one's respiration traveling from the bottom of the lungs to the top of the cranium via the thorax. It is the reason we elevate our thorax when we breathe profoundly to allow oxygen into our lungs and fill them. We frequently soothe our nervous system and reduce anxiety and tension.

By inhaling up and out, however, all of your positive energy or prana is expelled into the air. If you exhale, you will not benefit from fortifying your chakras. However, if your chakras are already robust and well-balanced, you may choose to exhale.

NOTE: For abdominal respiration, visualize and perform the opposite. Instead of inhaling and exhaling, drag your breath downwards and inwards, then deep into your abdomen.

In some cases, there are chest breathers and others who are abdominal breathers. If you classify yourself as a chest-breather, attempt to minimize your chest-lifting. Permit your abdomen to deflate as you exhale. More practice will enable you to master the technique, even if it is initially challenging. It is also acceptable to elevate your torso, so long as your stomach is moving quickly.

Some individuals have a propensity to contain their stomachs, specifically when they are motivated to appear slender. They unknowingly harbor powerful emotions in the abdominal region, which later manifests as second chakra issues. The storage of unwelcome emotions is deeply embedded within our organisms. These denied and unacknowledged emotions manifest themselves as maladies in the future.

People who have experienced trauma may find it difficult, frightening, or unpleasant to exercise abdominal breathing, and it is essential for those who experience difficulty to seek professional counseling.

Methods for Practicing Belly Breathing

First, breathe in deeply and deeply into the lower abdomen. Watch your stomach elevate to improve concentration. You can also concentrate on the palms you placed on your abdomen. If you continue to practice, you will no longer need to position your palms in your abdomen; however, if you appreciate the practice more with them there, that is acceptable.

Make sure you are retaining your breath in your abdomen when exhaling and your palms and midsection retract towards your spine. Do not allow your prana to escape; instead, draw the vital force into your body.

Imagine and visualize that you are filling a store with each breath you inhale, and also imagine exhaling while keeping your remaining breath in your abdomen, to help you fill your stomach quickly.

These are the only steps necessary to master the abdominal breathing techniques. Always ensure that you have taken at least 10 breaths to thoroughly recover. If you are accustomed to yoga breathing, abdominal breathing may be difficult because you are accustomed to inhaling a small amount of oxygen. You can simply attempt to breathe normally and practice abdominal breathing as time passes.

At least once or twice per day, particularly when you sense your body and mind lagging, practice abdominal breathing. This practice will increase your vitality, and you will notice a difference.

Sending Your Energy to Particular Chakra Areas After Collecting It In The Stomach

Once you have mastered how to collect your breath, energy, or prana in your abdomen, the next stage is to distribute it to other regions of your body.

This time, you will inhale and consolidate your breath or prana deep within the abdomen, and as you exhale, you will direct it to other regions of your body that you wish to heal, imagining this as you practice.

Practicing energy distribution is especially important if you are unwell, injured, or trapped. If you have a problem with your larynx, for example, you will direct your life force energy to your pharynx, and you will observe changes immediately. If you want to experience more compassion and affection, direct your exhalation over your heart, down your breastbone, and up into your larynx.

Also, when any part of your body is caught, such as your shoulders or hip, inhale deeply into your abdomen and exhale while sending energy or prana to your blocked shoulder or hip. You won't have to wait long before noticing changes.

Visualizing how to contain your breath in your abdomen and send it as energy to various regions of the body may appear challenging at first, but it will become simpler with practice. This is the fundamental rule when exercising respiration techniques to heal your chakras.

You can also use the following step-by-step respiration technique to heal your prana.

Cross your legs, ensure that your lips are lightly sealed, and breathe through your nostrils. Place your hands together and elevate them above your head.

Inhale as much air as possible while inhaling profoundly into the abdomen. You may choose to close or open your eyes, but in either case, visualize absorbing as much light as possible as it travels through your eyes, cranium, face, and ears.

When your airways are filled, prana fills them as well. Close your eyes, regardless of whether they were open or closed, and concentrate your awareness between them. Create a sphere of dazzling, concentrated light at your point of focus, between your eyebrows. You may encounter electrical flashes or sparkles; however, you should never lose focus, continue to concentrate, and remain calm.

As you exhale, observe the radiance dissipate to other body parts that require healing or balancing. Perform the exercise a minimum of 10 to 15 times.

Our body is constantly fueled by the energy we breathe in. In addition to the air we breathe, oxygen also comes from the food we consume, the water we drink, and the sun. These breathing techniques enable us to utilize the abundant prana in our bodies and heal our chakras. Additionally, we rehabilitate our spiritual being, spirits, and minds. By healing our chakras through these breathing techniques, we prevent any physical discomfort or illness. We also give our lives meaning, live in harmony with others, make prudent decisions, and have excellent relationships.

Improve Your Spiritual Vision Using The Third Eye Chakra

Third Eye Chakra consists of

The third eye chakra, or Ajna, is located between the eyebrows, in the region of the third eye. It consists of the pituitary gland, cranium, eyes, and lower portion of the brain. This is an intense yet undetectable third eye. In addition, this is the center of instinct. Ajna takes you inward, where it will assist and direct you if you allow it. An activated third eye chakra can facilitate unique perception, expanded creative energy, clairvoyance, and representation.

Your reality is perceived through the five senses that God has endowed you with. Indeed, prior to entering the womb, you heard your mother's voice and pulse, as well as muffled noises from the outside world. You experienced contact, flavor, and even light. In addition, from the moment of birth, you have attributed your experiences to what you perceive through the faculties. You have learned to trust your senses regarding what you can taste, smell, touch, see, and hear. In spite of the fact that sense discernment is fantastic for context, it prevents you from expanding your awareness.

Once upon a time, you had to rely on your instinct and inner knowing. Before modern innovation, we had to rely on natural cues and a more primitive sense to guide us. People possess an instinctive sense, similar to how avian creatures can predict when a storm will strike or how rodents know when it's time to stock up on food for the winter. We have just increased the distance between it and our ability to trust it.

Your physical faculties can provide clues regarding how to follow your intuition. These fragments of information are obtained through your senses. You have a tendency to disregard something that is not evident. The good news is that you can find out how to trust these pieces of information and make smarter decisions based on your intuition. Record your successful decisions to demonstrate that your instincts guided you in the correct direction. Remember that, like the animals in the wilderness, you have always possessed this intuition; you simply need to rediscover it.

In addition, the Third Eye aids in perceiving all surrounding circumstances and is the key to gaining insight and regulating the Life Force energies. In addition to contemplating and working with the chakra's energies, colors, images, and emotions, you will gain an internal understanding of the divine through the chakra. This is a definitive force location for healing others, and it allows you to Astral Projection or voluntarily interact with your etheric body.

In addition, you can use your internal sense to seek guidance in order to make the best decisions. Taking into account your psyche, perceptiveness, and sense of self, you are currently incorporating your spirit into the fundamental decision-making process. Generally, as you swung to the third chakra in the range of the sun-based plexus to guide you with comfort or distress, you will pay attention to an intuition or an unobtrusive feeling propelling you forward or holding you back. In the event that you are conflicted, request that your instincts be activated so that you can make the best decision.

Indicator of a Balanced Brow Chakra:

A person with a healthy, balanced, and robust chakra possesses both a keen intellect and robust natural abilities. Many could also refer to this as wisdom. Typically, they have a good creative spirit and can envisage things well. A consistently robust third eye chakra provides the ability to manage all situations. When this chakra is fully developed, a man will have expanded spiritual awareness and knowledge, as well as the potential to foresee what others cannot. Words that may be used to describe a man with a healthy, balanced, clear third eye chakra include wise, instinctive, clear, astute, perceptive, and extremely mindful.

Remove the Imbalances from the Third Eye Chakra

To activate the third eye chakra and establish a connection with your inner self, the following techniques must be utilized.

Meditation

Ajna, like other spiritual chakras, is most effectively adjusted through meditation. In addition, it operates on the principle of reflection. Beginners frequently report a trembling sensation in the third eye or compare it to a cerebral discomfort. A trembling or pulsating sensation around the area of the third eye during or after meditation indicates that this chakra is being unblocked.

Brahmari

Brahmari, also known as honey bee breath, is a phenomenal Pranayama breathing technique. Bring both palms to the face. Place your index and middle finger over your eyes. Permit the index fingers to rest on the brow line and the pinkies to rest beneath the cheekbones. With your fingertips, cover your ears. Take a deep inhalation and exhale the word AUM with the accent on the "M" sound while producing a honey-bee-like murmuring sound. Do this for at least two minutes. It reduces cranial pressure and endeavors to activate the third eye chakra.

Asnas

Any yoga asana in which the third eye chakra is depressed is a good one for the sixth chakra. Try the following position:

Child's posture-Dolphin pose (Balasana)

Precious stones and gemstones

These crystals are utilized to regulate the third eye chakra.

Amethyst

Lapis lazuli Azurite

Third eye centers affirmation

These are the assertions of this chakra:

I have a quick and nimble mind; I envision the beauty of this world and the kindness that surrounds me; I embrace the wisdom that surrounds me; and I am completely receptive to spiritual awareness.

Go star-gazing

This strategy entails the technique of stargazing and allowing the majesty of the constellations to activate your third eye.

Imagine your cranium as an expanding balloon. Allow it to float upright, positioning your ears above your shoulders. Perform this frequently to prepare and maintain a healthy spinal arrangement.

The Relationship Between The Throat Chakra

As demonstrated by ancient cultures, certain vibrations and sounds correspond to the distinct shading vibrations of the chakras. What does it mean to interface? It is a tendency that is easier to experience than to describe. Assume you are endeavoring to associate larynx erosion with, for example, the distance between the eyebrows. Prior to everything else, they are concurrently conscious. At that point, a natural reverberation occurs between the two.

The region between the eyebrows seems to fluctuate in tandem with the pharynx erosion. At that time, a "blending" occurs. The erosion of the pharynx combines with the slant between the eyebrows. There is a correspondence between the larynx and the Shakra in terms of vitality. That is what 'interfacing' implies.

Connection

Following a fundamental yet vital experience, the impression of the Shakra quickly becomes more specific and substantial. This outcome is unambiguous and prompt. The effect of larynx massaging is to 'give shape' or make objects more significant. Along these lines, whenever the larynx grating connects with a chakra or other spiritual organ, the organ becomes more distinct. The larynx exposes things; it reveals them.

A comparable effect will be observed when removing ars. You must first cultivate your inner strength and draw during the time you are not seeing. Then, a few activities will demonstrate how your perception of nonphysical coronas and atmospheres is immediately enhanced by combining pharynx erosion and vsion. The hues and tones will demonstrate that you are fundamentally "denser" and more substantial.

Throat erosion can similarly be used to establish a connection between various forms of vitality. Not only can you associate the grinding with the Shakra or any other organ of vitality, but you can also upgrade the association between different organs of vitality and connect them via contact.

We observe that through our voice, we convey our thoughts and emotions, thereby giving them a more characterized structure. You will realize that larynx grinding makes the Shakra more recognizable, as if it were forming it. You will tune into your Shakra, and as soon as you begin the vocal grating, the

Shakra will be seen more clearly and with greater gravity.

How do Chakras work?

According to an old proverb, a healthy spirit can only reside in a healthy body. The majority of people may view chakras as something very spiritual, perhaps only accessible to enlightened individuals or those born with psychic abilities. And while engaging the upper chakras can indeed give you a greater sense of connection to the universe and a broader spiritual domain, chakras also have physical purposes – particularly the lower chakras.

Many believe that each chakra is a junction between the physical and spiritual bodies. The body is therefore very essential; the fact that we are all composed of energy does not diminish the significance of our physical health. In fact, mental disorders such as anxiety and depression can have a strong correlation with physical ailments. This is why we will begin by examining the lower chakras, which will guide you toward physical body healing first and foremost. Then, as we ascend the scale, we will unravel emotional and mental difficulties. Finally, we will examine the upper chakras, which serve as a bridge between our world and the spiritual world.

Yoga is a beneficial practice that connects the body, mind, and spirit through breathing techniques and physical exercise; therefore, this book will provide you with yoga exercises as you strive to clear each chakra. Please keep in mind that yoga should never be painful, so if you are in pain or have experienced injuries in the past, be mindful of these and cease if something feels too unpleasant. You should also incorporate the poses from this book into a larger practice, such as a sun salutation, rather than attempting each pose individually.

A concise overview of chakra healing

The term chakras means "wheel" or "circle" and its origin is Sanskrit. Sometimes translated as "the wheel of life" The concept of respiration channels within the body was first mentioned in the Upanishads, a compilation of texts containing the most significant philosophical ideas of Hinduism. It is difficult to pinpoint the precise date, but many sources concur that the Upanishads of the seventh to eighth centuries BCE describe the earliest conceptions of an energy or life force that permeates all living things.

The term "chakra" originated between the second century BCE and the second century CE. Since then, the concept has evolved in a number of directions, but the most prevalent belief today is that the human body contains seven chakras, with the lower ones located at the base of the vertebrae and ascending to the summit of the cranium. However, the difficulty for Western comprehension when discussing chakras is that, as pure energy, chakras cannot be located tangibly.

a rainbow of chakras

The prevalent metaphor for the functioning of chakras is that your body is composed of so much water, which flows through you daily. The body emits a spectrum of seven colors when combined with light, with each color representing a distinct chakra. When the water in your body becomes stagnant — that is, when there is little or no movement — a rainbow cannot be ignited, and your internal environment becomes noxious. Frequently, a dramatic shift in perception is required. A declaration to yourself that you want this change to occur no matter what is a good starting point for the change; you may then sense the energies within your body begin to shift.

What occurs when the chakras are obstructed or out of balance?

The chakra points are always active, but they can be either insufficiently or excessively active. For instance, if your root or base chakra is blocked, your heart chakra may become overactive to compensate. You may not feel grounded, but you develop strong attachments to others and your emotions fluctuate significantly. Even if you are seeking spiritual enlightenment, which is commonly associated with the crown chakra, or you wish to develop a stronger intuition, you cannot achieve these goals without first releasing any obstructions in your lower chakras. To determine whether or not there are obstructions, you must always begin with your root chakra and work your way up. The purpose of this book is to assist you in obtaining an equilibrium between all of your chakras, which will hopefully lead to a balance in your body and in your life.

In a broader sense

Despite the fact that this book is a practical guide to healing chakras to enhance your physical reality, it is fascinating to speculate on what other implications this may have. Ilchi Lee Sedona, who has practiced chakra healing for decades, believes that by healing chakras, we can repair the Earth as a whole – the primary imbalances we observe in ourselves are also the primary imbalances in humanity as a whole. Another theory holds that as humanity has evolved over the years, it has also evolved through the seven chakras, first developing the concept of time, then moving up to the chakras that govern reason and science, and that we are currently in the realm of the chakra that governs universal love and self-reflection. It is therefore not surprising that self-help books are gaining popularity and that individuals are turning inward for answers and healing, assuming responsibility for their own happiness.

The Significance Of Energy Hubs

As previously indicated, the Sanskrit term chakra signified a circle or a wheel. Nonetheless, it is essential to consider that these circles represent energy centers within the body. The subtle form of the body serves as the foundation for chakras, and the subtle body itself exists in an immaterial form. The subtle body is said to be constituted of energy itself, whereas the physical body is made up of flesh and bones. The energy system is called a chakra or a wheel due to its rotating nature and rotational factor. The seven varieties of chakras listed previously each have their own properties, identities, and functions. If chakras are viewed as a prism, they appear to divide the light entering our body into distinct colors at various body levels. This is the reason chakras are associated with specific hues. The need to study chakras arises so that individuals can conquer their chakras in order to unify their personal attributes and recognize the soul-embedded, concealed characteristics in their bodies. By the time a person recognizes his chakras, he is aware of his own characteristics and has attained a spiritual level that fosters self-awareness.

Fifth Chapter - Fourth Chakra

The fourth chakra of the human organism, Anahata, is also known as the heart chakra. Its symbol is comprised of a hexagram (two intersecting triangles representing the union of male and female) and an exterior circle with twelve green petals, and its complexity follows the same ascendant path.

Since Anahata is associated with the color green, anything of this hue can increase the energy flow at this level of the body. As the lungs are located in the center of the chest, close to the heart, any imbalances can cause heart and respiratory problems, such as elevated blood pressure, chest discomfort, and heart attacks. Due to its proximity to the thymus, any imbalance also effects the immune system, the body's primary defense. In the end, cardiac disease is the leading cause of mortality. Thus, it is essential to maintain this chakra with the utmost care and appease its energetic requirements. The best methods to achieve this are by taking long treks in nature and spending time with friends and family. Eliminating significant sources of tension is an additional factor in ensuring that your Anahata is functioning correctly.

The heart chakra is what motivates you to be compassionate, cordial, and empathetic with others on an emotional level. It is what we refer to as kindness. The desire to find the positive in everything and everyone, and to always choose to see the full glass, originates deep within the fourth chakra. The sensation of affection, the highest emotion a human being is capable of producing, likely originates here.

Balance implies that a person is equally capable of giving and receiving affection, just as energy flows to and from each chakra in the body. If few resources are available and those few resources are consumed by negative emotions and anxious thoughts, the likelihood of love occurring is minimal. Self-acceptance, forgiveness, and compassion serve as the foundations of love's pyramidal structure.

As we can see, the structure and function of the entire chakra system assigns lower levels to unadulterated sexuality and a higher level to love. This does not imply that one is more essential than the other. On a scale of importance, they are equally weighted, but diverting energy to the upper levels requires significantly more effort. It is comparable to the pressure necessary for water to ascend a conduit. The greater the required ascent, the greater the imposed pressure must be.

Tibetan Buddhism views Anahata as the dwelling place of the indestructible red/white drop, which is responsible for transporting our consciousness to the next existence. This presence teaches those who believe in reincarnation and eternal existence lived in different bodies that the body is more than just a conveyance. A minimum portion of it is immortal and transcends from existence to existence. This optimism does justice to the ancient Latin adage, "The end of life is not the end of love."

Fifth Chakra

The fifth chakra, known as Viduddha in Sanskrit, is located in the pharynx region and marks the progression of the chakra system towards the cranium, the uppermost part of the body. The fifth chakra is represented by a downward triangle that includes and is included by adjacent circles. The exterior circle is adorned with sixteen petals of turquoise. Blue, the fifth color of the visible light spectrum, has a significant relationship with the pharynx chakra. Any form of blue in your daily life can stimulate this energetic center and bring it into a state of equilibrium.

The Viduddha is firmly connected to the body's primary communication channels. The larynx, an organ included in the fifth chakra's influence area, produces the voice. All types of infections, disorders related to the way hormones are released in the body, hyperactivity, and any mouth, mandible, tongue, or neck issues are physical effects of imbalance. The affected area may extend to the shoulders.

The fifth chakra can affect a person's openness to change, transformation, and personal restoration. The ability to communicate and express oneself naturally and effectively is determined by the energy contained and released in Viduddha. You can identify individuals with an imbalance at this level based on their behavior and language. Withholding one's thoughts, speaking softly, or being unable to communicate with others are all significant indications of anxiety. Those who have attained complete control over the energy flow at this chakra enjoy enhanced concentration, creativity, ease of expression, and artistic perspective.

The "muscle" of the vocal chakra can be exercised through singing, engaging in fruitful dialogues, and delivering profound addresses.

www.ingramcontent.com/pod-product-compliance
Lightning Source LLC
Chambersburg PA
CBHW050253120526
44590CB00016B/2333